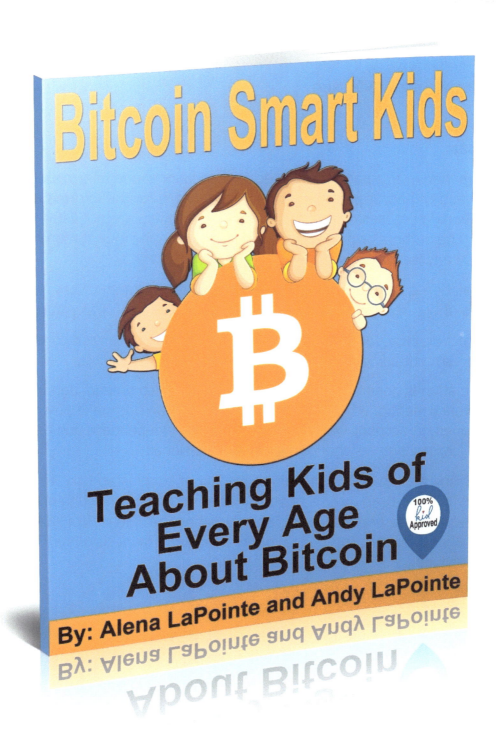

www.BitcoinSmartKids.com

Disclaimer:

The information in this book is provided for educational and informational purposes only. The author and/or publisher are not responsible for the information provided. It is for educational purposes only. The authors or publishers are not liable for errors and omission. The authors or publishers are not liable for any loss of money or other value incurred by anyone purchasing or reading this book.

The information is without any expressed or implied warranty of any kind, including warranties of accuracy, completeness, or recommendation for any purpose.

The information provided here is not intended to be and does not constitute financial advice, investment advice, trading advice or any other advice.

This information is general information and is not a recommendation to invest into any cryptocurrency mentioned or not mentioned. Please do not make any decision to invest, trade, or open an account without doing your own independent due diligence. Please consult a licensed professional or financial professional.

Risk Statement – Investing in and the trading of bitcoins and cryptocurrencies are extremely risky. You can lose all of your money very fast. Investing and trading Bitcoin and cryptocurrencies may not be suitable for all people. Please consult a licensed professional or financial professional prior to making any decision to invest, trade or open an account.

Welcome to the World of Bitcoin:

Hi! I am Satoshi Nakamoto. My name is pronounced as Sah-toe-she Na-Ka-Moto. My students call me Satoshi.

I will be teaching you about Bitcoin. I invented Bitcoin to be a form of digital cash or electronic money.

However, Satoshi Nakamoto is not my real name. Nobody really knows my real identity. I am the unknown person that created Bitcoin in 2008.

This book will introduce you to the world of Bitcoin and many of its digital cash friends.

Bitcoin is fun! You will have a great time learning about this new kind of digital money and how it works.

What is Bitcoin?

Bitcoin is a form of electronic money. It is like the kind of money used to buy and sell stuff in videos games.

Unlike virtual money used only in video games, Bitcoin can be used to buy things online and offline.

Bitcoin can be used to buy food, clothes, books, computers, smartphones and nearly everything the money in your pocket can buy.

With Bitcoin, you can buy many of the things you want. You can also send Bitcoins to friends or family members.

Bitcoin is Digital Cash

Let me explain what I mean. Below is a $1 bill.

You can buy stuff with paper money. You can buy clothes, food, videos games or go to the movies.

Let's say your friend, Ryan, is selling a candy bar for $1. You give Ryan the $1 and he gives you the candy bar.

You can use digital cash the same way! When you buy something with digital cash, you pay with your smartphone. Now, let's buy some candy from Ryan using Bitcoin. You can send Bitcoin from your phone to Ryan's phone. When Ryan gets the Bitcoin, he will give you the candy bar.

Bitcoin is "Peer-to-Peer" Digital Cash

Just like cash, you can send bitcoin to a friend or a peer (another word for a person). You don't need someone else, such as a bank, to send money to a peer. That is why Bitcoin is often called a peer-to-peer system.

If you want to give your friend (a peer) a $1 bill, you remove the $1 bill from your wallet and give it to your friend. Bitcoin allows you to do the same thing, but with digital cash, using a smartphone or computer.

Bitcoin is Like Email

Email allows you to send messages online. You can send messages and photos to anyone in the world.

The Bitcoin network allows you to send digital cash to anyone in the world from your smartphone or computer.

Bitcoin's Street Address

You send Bitcoins using a specific Bitcoin address. Just like at your home, you have a very special street address.

Nobody else in the entire world has the same street address as you. Bitcoin works the very same way.

A Bitcoin address is made up of a lot of letters and numbers.

Don't worry, you don't have to remember the Bitcoin address. The special Bitcoin software on your smartphone or computer remembers it for you.

Here is what a Bitcoin address looks like:

Bitcoin Address:

12CFcbzB2Fff4Ad3wseZwDGFT5g6ASZdFw

When you send an email or a letter in the mail, you send it to a specific address. To send bitcoin from your smartphone, all you need to do is enter the specific Bitcoin address you want to send bitcoin to.

To get bitcoin, give your Bitcoin address to your friend.

How to Keep Your Bitcoins Safe

You keep your bitcoins safe by storing them in a Bitcoin wallet.

Your Bitcoin wallet can be stored on your smartphone or on your computer. If you store your Bitcoin wallet on your smartphone, you can take your Bitcoin with you anywhere in the world.

The Pennies, Nickels, Dimes and Quarters of Bitcoin

Dollars can be divided into smaller denominations: quarters, dimes, nickels and pennies.

The smallest amount of money a $1 bill can be divided into are pennies. 100 pennies equal $1.

100 Pennies $1 Dollar

Just like a $1 bill, Bitcoin can be spent in smaller amounts.

These smaller denominations are called micropayments. You can send one whole bitcoin or smaller amounts to anyone in the world.

Bitcoin is a Cryptocurrency

Let me introduce you to Bitcoin's family. Bitcoin is part of the family called cryptocurrency. Cryptocurrency is pronounced (krip-toh-kur-uh-n-see).

I know cryptocurrency may sound like a funny name for a family. It may even sound like a big and scary word, but it is not. It's just two words put together.

Bitcoin is the big brother of the of the cryptocurrency family. There are a bunch of other digital cash coins that are Bitcoin's friends, siblings, and cousins. Bitcoin is the oldest of all cryptocurrencies. Sometimes he is even called the **King of Cryptocurrencies.**

All cryptocurrencies have a special symbol. Bitcoin's symbol is the **fancy** ☐. All of the other family members have their own symbol or logo.

You can see this logo on the different coins. Let me introduce you to some of the other family members of the cryptocurrency family. First is Ethereum, also called Ether. Notice how the symbol is different from the Bitcoin symbol.

Next, we have Ripple…

Here is a coin called Stellar...

Finally, let me introduce you to the coin called Cardano...

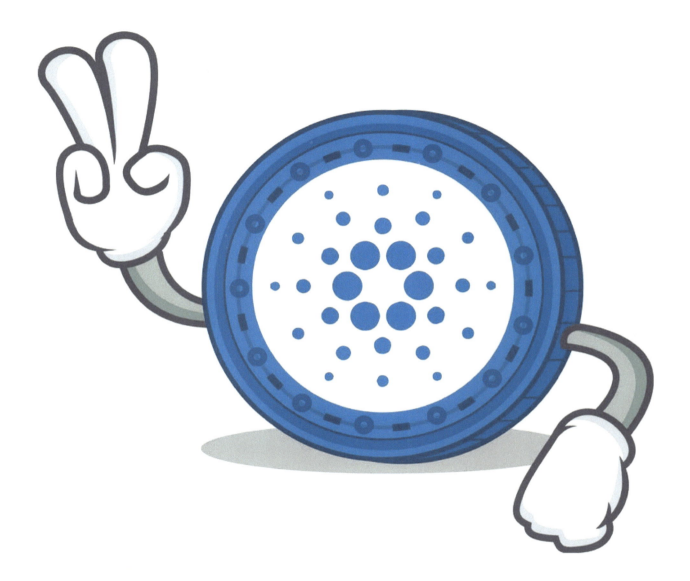

Each coin does something a little different than the other coins. Some coins are built to go very fast in sending money, while others offer special ways of doing things.

Where Do Bitcoins Come From? How are Bitcoins Made?

You can make a Bitcoin. That's right, you can make a Bitcoin from your very own computer. Just like mining gold from the ground, bitcoins can be mined. You use a very special computer program to mine Bitcoins.

You can also mine other members of the cryptocurrency family with your computer. There are a lot of bitcoins friends, siblings and cousins you can mine.

How to Earn Bitcoin

You can earn Bitcoin. Bitcoins can be earned by selling something or working for Bitcoin. Some companies pay Bitcoin to people who work for them.

How to Buy Bitcoin

You can also buy Bitcoins from a Bitcoin Exchange. A bitcoin exchange is a place you can send paper/traditional money and exchange it for bitcoin and other members of the cryptocurrency family.

The cryptocurrency family is very large. Here are a few of the other members of the cryptocurrency family. All of the different coins have different symbols or logos.

Saving Bitcoin, Spending Bitcoin and Investing in Bitcoin

You can do a lot with Bitcoin. You can buy stuff with Bitcoin, you can save and invest into Bitcoin for the future. Just like owning a stock, some people hold onto Bitcoin as an investment. But, keep in mind, just like a stock the price of Bitcoin and other members of the cryptocurrency family can go up and down every day.

PRICE DECREASE

PRICE INCREASE

As the price of Bitcoin goes up, it is worth more money. As the price of Bitcoin goes down, the less money you have.

Thank You from Satoshi

I hope you enjoyed learning about Bitcoin. I also hope you enjoyed learning about some of the other members of the cryptocurrency family.

I wish you the very best and bright future.

Sincerely,

Satoshi Nakamoto

Before you go…

Bitcoin would like to share a few additional places your parents can go to and learn more about Bitcoin and cryptocurrencies.

Check with your parents before you visit any website.

Check out Bitcoin learning videos at:

CryptoLearningVideos.com

Learn more about Bitcoin and other members of the cryptocurrency family at:

CryptoWisdom.com

Check out MoneySmartTeens.com to learn more about money ideas for kids and teens.

www.ingramcontent.com/pod-product-compliance
Lightning Source LLC
LaVergne TN
LVHW060202050326
832903LV00016B/348